*To our mothers, Geneva Hewitt and Lucille
Morrison, the inspiring cooks in our lives,
and to our families for their love, support,
enthusiasm, and unfailing belief in us
and our abilities to write cookbooks.*

CONTENTS

Fiber

Fruit

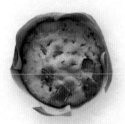

ACKNOWLEDGMENTS

We have had many challenging experiences throughout our years of writing and publishing cookbooks, but we can say that it has been truly rewarding as it has given us the opportunity to work together and collaborate with many wonderful people. We specifically wish to thank the following:

Our mothers, Geneva Hewitt and Lucille Morrison, who inspired our love of cooking and our writing endeavors.

The staff at the Tattered Cover Book Store, who a few years ago suggested that we provide them with a muffin cookbook. We truly appreciate their encouragement during our "great muffin project."

Our families, L.G, Bob, Heidi, Wade, Toni, Wendi, Shawn, and Heather, for "enjoying" muffins for breakfast, lunch, dinner, snacks, picnics, etc.

Photographer Sheena Bates, who turned an ordinary muffin cookbook into a work of art.

Editor Michelle Branson, for her support and tremendous enthusiasm for this project. And to the great staff at Gibbs Smith, for believing in our muffin cookbook and working with us to complete it.

· INTRODUCTION ·

When we agreed to write the first edition of this muffin book, we realized the only thing we knew about muffins was how much we loved them. With the help of friends and family, we spent a year researching, experimenting with, and tasting hundreds of muffins until we came up with the best possible options. After a recipe was selected, it was sent to Texas to be tested in home kitchens at a lower altitude. Fortunately, we found that altitude had little effect on our recipes if the oven was preheated and an adjustment was made in cooking time (see Helpful Hints, page 10). From these options we selected a variety of recipes for you that are not only easy to make, but also taste delicious.

During our "great muffin project" we came to the realization that in many ways our approaches to baking differed. Mother Earth Cyndi cooks from scratch and is one of those incredibly organized cooks who does those wonderfully domesticated things in the kitchen. She is the one who grows her own fruits and vegetables, always has cookies in the cookie jar, and can feed an army of teenagers in fifteen minutes. Georgie, the Queen of Easy, who thinks of herself as an "efficient assembler" when it comes to cooking, buys most everything canned, sliced, diced, and shredded from the grocery store. She thinks it helps the economy and, most importantly, leaves time for curling up with a good book.

In spite of our differences, we found that both of us have a real desire to write cookbooks that are used, not just shelved. We wanted *Muffins* to be one of those books. Sitting at the kitchen table one afternoon, we outlined the features necessary for a unique, easy-to-use cookbook for the Cyndis and Georgies of the world. It didn't take long to decide that a cookbook, to be well used, must have recipes with clear instructions and basic pantry ingredients, include baking tips, appeal to the new cook as well as to the most experienced, and look fantastic.

We feel that the collection of recipes we ultimately included in *Muffins* and the format we chose to use have made this muffin book one of a kind. Not only is it a wonderful addition to your own cookbook library, it also makes an excellent gift for any Cyndi or Georgie.

Enjoy your *Muffins* and happy baking!

· HELPFUL HINTS ·

Substitutions we found useful

- Replace buttermilk by souring 1 cup milk with 1 tablespoon lemon juice or white vinegar.

- Buttermilk and sour cream are interchangeable.

- Egg substitutes can be used in place of eggs. The package will state equivalents. Eggs and egg substitutes should be used at or close to room temperature.

- Interchange ingredients, e.g., apricots for peaches, dried cranberries for dried cherries, honey for ½ the molasses, light brown sugar for dark brown sugar (the difference is the amount of molasses mixed with sugar).

- For cream-style corn, substitute whole kernel corn plus ½ cup milk, buttermilk, or plain yogurt. Add a pinch of baking soda.

- For fewer calories, use vegetable spray on pans.

- Using oil in place of shortening in equal amounts is a matter of preference. With all the hoopla about trans fats, we generally substitute oil in most of our baking.

- Decreasing or omitting salt in recipes is okay. Salt is a flavor enhancer, but isn't always healthy.

- Sugar substitutes can replace equal amounts of granulated sugar, however, we have found that using equal amounts makes muffins too sweet, so we cut the amount by ⅓. Baked products won't brown as well with sugar substitutes.

- Oats and quick oats can be interchanged. Old-fashioned or steel-cut oats may make the muffin grainier.

- Using more mashed ripe bananas in a recipe than called for is okay without changing the end result too much. Muffins will be moister and heavier. Ripe bananas can be frozen until ready to use. When slightly thawed, they are easy to remove from the peel.

- Make an oat-bran substitute by pulsing regular oats in a food processor until finely ground.

- Muffin recipe batter can be baked in loaf pans to make quick bread if desired. A longer baking time is required.

- Tasty additions to sweet muffins include baking chips, fruits, dried fruits, nuts, extracts or liqueurs, and spices.

- Flavorful additions to savory muffins include hard cheeses, mustards, herbs, hot pepper sauce, Worcestershire sauce, chopped vegetables, nuts, or seeds.

Baking tips

- Preheating the oven is necessary for muffins to rise properly.

- Muffin tins come in a variety of sizes. Adjust baking time accordingly.

- If one or two muffin cups are not filled with batter, fill the empty cups ½ full with water for more even baking.

- Paper liners can be used rather than spraying cups with nonstick cooking spray.

- Muffin cups filled ⅔ full will have a flatter top; muffin cups filled ¾ full will be more rounded and require slightly more baking time.

- Baking times vary with different ovens and locations. Adjust baking time accordingly.

- Check muffins close to end of stated baking time. When making miniature muffins, cut baking time in half.

- Note that convection ovens take less time for baking because of circulating air. For example, a convection oven setting at 325 degrees F equals the standard oven setting of 350 degrees F.

- Mixing a small amount of flour or powdered sugar with berries or nuts prevents them from sinking to the bottom of the muffins.

- When muffins are done, they will spring back when touched, or a toothpick inserted in the center will come out clean, and they will be lightly browned.

- Muffins will be easier to remove if they are left in the pan for 4–5 minutes before removing them to a rack to cool. If necessary, loosen edges of muffins with a knife.

Other tidbits

- Sifting flour is no longer necessary. Simply measure and combine dry ingredients.

- Usually stir wet ingredients into dry ingredients until just moistened. The key to a good muffin texture is not to overstir the batter.

- Butter should be at room temperature or softened in the microwave for 5–10 seconds before using.

- Most muffins can be frozen for a short period of time. Wad up a piece of barely damp paper towel and lay on top of muffins inside the container. This keeps the muffins from taking on so much of a freezer taste.

- Toast sesame seeds or nuts in a skillet sprayed with nonstick cooking spray, stirring often and watching carefully as process goes quickly once heated.

- Dip measuring spoons in oil or a cup of hot water before measuring honey, molasses, or corn syrup to prevent sticking.

fiber

· GOLDEN BRAN ·

MAKES 12 MUFFINS

Golden raisins add wonderful flavor and texture to these fiber-filled muffins. They are delicious with a dollop of honey butter.

1 cup buttermilk
2 eggs, slightly beaten
¼ cup melted and cooled, lightly
   salted butter or margarine
¼ cup canola oil
2½ tablespoons honey
1½ tablespoons molasses
1½ cups crumbled bran flakes
½ cup unprocessed bran
1 cup whole-wheat flour
¼ cup firmly packed
   dark brown sugar
1 teaspoon baking powder
1 teaspoon baking soda
¼ teaspoon salt
¾ cup golden raisins

Preheat oven to 400 degrees F. Spray muffin cups with nonstick cooking spray.

In large bowl, stir together buttermilk, eggs, butter, oil, honey, and molasses until blended. Stir in bran flakes and bran, and let stand 1–2 minutes, or until cereal is softened.

In another large bowl, stir flour, brown sugar, baking powder, baking soda, and salt together. Make a well in the center of the dry ingredients. Add bran mixture and stir just to combine. Stir in raisins.

Fill muffin cups ¾ full. Bake for 15–20 minutes. Cool for 5 minutes, remove from pan, and serve warm.

Note Store in airtight container at room temperature for 2–3 days. These muffins freeze well.

· CARROT & BRAN ·

MAKES 24 MUFFINS

This is Cyndi's favorite muffin. She is usually a chocolate lover, but she really appreciates the spicy, moist, whole-grain texture of these muffins.

3 cups flour
1 teaspoon baking soda
2 teaspoons baking powder
½ teaspoon salt
1 tablespoon cinnamon
2 cups crumbled bran flakes
4 eggs
1 ½ cups canola oil
1 ¼ cups firmly packed
   dark brown sugar
¼ cup molasses
3 cups finely grated carrots
1 cup raisins or currants

Preheat oven to 350 degrees F. Spray muffin cups with nonstick cooking spray.

In large bowl, combine flour, baking soda, baking powder, salt, and cinnamon. Stir in bran flakes and set aside.

In another large bowl, beat eggs, oil, brown sugar, and molasses. Stir in carrots and raisins. Combine egg and flour mixtures, stirring until just moist.

Fill muffin cups ¾ full. Bake for 20 minutes. Cool for 5 minutes and remove from pan.

Variation For a different taste treat, use light brown sugar, substitute honey for ½ of the molasses, and add nuts.

· BANANA BRAN ·

MAKES 12 MUFFINS

Do you always have one banana that overripens before you can eat it? Freeze it each time, and when you have enough for a recipe, thaw and bake something yummy. Try serving these muffins with slices of fresh banana for an extra pop of flavor.

1 ⅓ cups All-Bran cereal
1 cup mashed banana
6 tablespoons canola oil
⅓ cup honey
¼ cup molasses
1 egg, room temperature
1 teaspoon fresh lemon juice
1 cup plus 2 tablespoons flour
1 ¼ teaspoons baking powder
½ teaspoon cinnamon
1 teaspoon baking soda
½ teaspoon salt
½ cup chopped dates, optional

Preheat oven to 400 degrees F. Spray muffin cups with nonstick cooking spray.

Mix cereal, banana, oil, honey, molasses, egg, and lemon juice in medium bowl.

Combine flour, baking powder, cinnamon, baking soda, and salt in large bowl. Stir in dates if using.

Make a well in the center of the dry ingredients. Add banana mixture to well and stir until just blended. The batter will be lumpy.

Fill muffin cups ¾ full. Bake for 15–20 minutes. Cool for 5 minutes and remove from pan.

· EASY BRAN ·

The bran flakes in these muffins are crunchy when first baked,
but become chewy when reheated. They taste great both ways.

2 tablespoons shortening
3 tablespoons sugar
1 egg
¾ cup milk
1 cup bran flakes
1 cup flour
2 teaspoons baking powder
½ teaspoon salt

Preheat oven to 375 degrees F. Spray muffin cups with nonstick cooking spray.

Cream shortening and sugar in large bowl until light and fluffy. Add egg and beat well.

Stir in milk, add bran flakes, and mix well.

In small bowl, combine flour, baking powder, and salt and stir into bran mixture just until moistened.

Fill muffin cups ⅔ full. Bake for 20–25 minutes. Cool for 5 minutes and remove from pan.

· LIGHT BRAN ·

MAKES 12 MUFFINS

The combination of wheat bran and oat bran gives these muffins a delicate texture. They are great served at breakfast with honey butter.

2 large eggs
¼ cup firmly packed
  light brown sugar
1 cup milk
¼ cup canola oil
1 ½ cups wheat-bran cereal
½ cup oat bran
½ cup flour
2 teaspoons baking powder

Preheat oven to 375 degrees F. Spray muffin cups with nonstick cooking spray.

Beat eggs and brown sugar in medium bowl until smooth. Whisk in milk and oil. Stir in wheat-bran cereal. Let stand at least 10 minutes.

Combine oat bran, flour, and baking powder in large bowl. Add wheat-bran mixture and stir just until dry ingredients are moistened.

Fill muffin cups ¾ full. Bake 20–25 minutes or until brown and firm in the center. Cool for 5 minutes and remove from pan.

Variation Brush muffins with maple syrup when removed from oven, or add ½ cup raisins or ½ cup walnuts to batter before baking.

· CHEDDAR BRAN ·

MAKES 12 MUFFINS

Serve these muffins warm with an herb-infused
butter to best experience the cheddar flavor.

1 cup whole bran
1 ¼ cups buttermilk or sour milk
¼ cup shortening
⅓ cup sugar
1 egg
1 ½ cups flour
1 ½ teaspoons baking powder
½ teaspoon salt
¼ teaspoon baking soda
1 cup shredded sharp
   cheddar cheese

Preheat oven to 400 degrees F. Spray
muffin cups with nonstick cooking spray.

In small bowl, soften bran in buttermilk.
In large bowl, cream shortening and
sugar until fluffy. Beat in egg.

In another bowl, combine flour, baking
powder, salt, and baking soda. Add to
creamed mixture alternately with bran
mixture. Stir in cheese.

Fill muffin cups ⅔ full. Bake for
15–20 minutes. Cool for 5 minutes
and remove from pan.

· HONEY BRAN ·

MAKES 12 MUFFINS

This muffin is a healthy choice, and can be made even
healthier when salt is omitted and egg substitute,
sunflower oil, and hard red spring-wheat bran is used.

1 cup boiling water
1 cup raisins or chopped dates
2 1/2 teaspoons baking soda
1 1/2 cups honey
2 3/4 cups flour
1/2 teaspoon salt
2 eggs
1/2 cup canola oil
2 cups buttermilk
3 1/2 to 4 cups unprocessed
   wheat bran

Preheat oven to 375 degrees F. Spray muffin cups with nonstick cooking spray.

In small bowl, pour boiling water over raisins or dates and add baking soda. Lightly mix honey, flour, salt, eggs, oil, buttermilk, and wheat bran together in a separate bowl. Add raisin mixture and stir until just moistened. If batter seems too thin, stir in remaining 1/2 cup wheat bran.

Fill muffin cups 3/4 full. Bake for 20 minutes. Cool for 5 minutes and remove from pan.

· WHOLE-WHEAT BRAN ·

MAKES 24 MUFFINS

Bet you can't eat just one of these wonderfully moist bran muffins.

3 cups crumbled bran flakes
½ cup canola oil
1 cup raisins
1 cup boiling water
2 eggs, lightly beaten
2 cups buttermilk
¼ cup molasses
2¼ cups whole-wheat flour
4 teaspoons sugar
2½ teaspoons baking soda
¼ teaspoon salt

Preheat oven to 400 degrees F. Spray muffin cups with nonstick cooking spray.

Combine bran flakes, oil, and raisins in large bowl and pour the boiling water over them. Set mixture aside to cool.

Combine eggs, buttermilk, and molasses in a small bowl. Add to cereal mixture.

Combine flour, sugar, baking soda, and salt in another small bowl and add to cereal mixture. Stir only enough to moisten dry ingredients. Cover and let stand at least 15 minutes, but 1 hour is preferred.

Fill muffin cups ¾ full. Bake for 15–20 minutes. Cool for 5 minutes and remove from pan.

· CARROT & ROSEMARY ·

MAKES 12 MUFFINS

The rosemary in this muffin recipe makes it quite unusual. The combination of slightly sweet currants and the herb flavor is delightful.

1 cup currants
1 ½ cups boiling water
½ cup olive oil
½ teaspoon vanilla
2 cups flour
1 cup whole-wheat flour
⅔ cup sugar
2 teaspoons baking soda
2 teaspoons crushed rosemary
2 cups grated carrots

Preheat oven to 375 degrees F. Spray muffin cups with nonstick cooking spray.

In small bowl, combine currants, boiling water, olive oil, and vanilla; set aside.

In large bowl, combine flours, sugar, baking soda, and rosemary. Make a well in the center of the dry ingredients. Add wet ingredients, stirring until moistened. Fold in carrots until evenly blended.

Fill muffin cups ⅔ full. Bake for 20-25 minutes. Cool for 5 minutes and remove from pan.

· WHOLE WHEAT ·

MAKES 12 MUFFINS

For an even healthier muffin, use egg substitute and reduce or omit salt.

2 cups whole-wheat flour
2 tablespoons firmly
  packed brown sugar
2 teaspoons baking powder
1 ½ teaspoons ground cinnamon
¼ teaspoon salt
1 egg, beaten
1 cup plus 2 tablespoons
  skim milk
3 tablespoons melted butter

Preheat oven to 400 degrees F. Spray muffin cups with nonstick cooking spray.

Combine flour, brown sugar, baking powder, cinnamon, and salt in large bowl and make a well in the center of the mixture.

Whisk egg, milk, and butter in small bowl. Add to dry ingredients, stirring just until moistened.

Fill muffin cups ⅔ full. Bake for 15–20 minutes. Cool for 5 minutes and remove from pan.

fruit

· TRUE-BLUE BERRY ·

MAKES 12 MUFFINS

The juice from the blueberries makes this a true-blue berry muffin.

¼ cup butter, melted
½ cup sugar
1 egg
1 ¼ cups flour
2 teaspoons baking powder
½ teaspoon salt
¼ cup milk
¾ cup canned blueberries,
  drained but not rinsed,
  saving ¼ cup juice

Preheat oven to 400 degrees F. Spray muffin cups with nonstick cooking spray.

Cream butter, sugar, and egg in large bowl.

Combine flour, baking powder, and salt in medium bowl.

Stir flour mixture into creamed mixture alternately with milk and juice from blueberries. Fold in blueberries.

Fill muffin cups ⅔ full. Bake for 20 minutes. Cool for 5 minutes and remove from pan.

· BLUEBERRY PINWHEEL ·

MAKES 12 MUFFINS

This muffin takes a little more time to prepare, but the end product is lovely. Mmmm good for breakfast, lunch, or dinner.

2 cups prepared biscuit mix
2 tablespoons sugar
2/3 cup milk
2 tablespoons grated orange zest
1/4 cup melted butter
1 can (15 ounces)
   blueberries, drained
1/2 teaspoon ground cinnamon
1/3 cup chopped nuts, of choice
1/3 cup firmly packed brown sugar

Preheat oven to 425 degrees F. Spray muffin cups with nonstick cooking spray.

In large bowl, combine biscuit mix and sugar. Stir in milk and orange zest just until moistened.

Knead about 10 times on a floured surface until dough is smooth. Roll out to a 10 x 18-inch rectangle. Brush dough with melted butter. Sprinkle blueberries, cinnamon, nuts, and brown sugar over dough.

Roll up like a jelly roll, starting at the 18-inch side. Cut roll into 12 equal pieces and place in muffin cups.

Bake for 15–20 minutes. Cool for 5 minutes and remove from pan.

· SAUCY BLUEBERRY-LEMON ·

These wonderfully tart creations melt in your mouth.

½ cup butter or margarine
½ cup sugar
2 eggs
2 cups flour
3 teaspoons baking powder
¼ teaspoon salt
⅓ cup milk
1 cup canned or thawed and
   drained frozen blueberries
1 lemon, finely zested

Sauce
¼ cup fresh lemon juice
⅓ cup sugar

Preheat oven to 350 degrees F. Spray muffin cups with nonstick cooking spray.

Cream butter, sugar, and eggs in a small bowl.

In large bowl, combine flour, baking powder, and salt. Add creamed mixture alternately with milk until mixed. Fold in blueberries and lemon zest.

Fill muffin cups ⅔ full. Bake for 25–30 minutes.

For the sauce, combine lemon juice and sugar in small pan and bring to a boil. Pour sauce evenly over top of hot muffins and serve.

· STATE FAIR BLUEBERRY ·

MAKES 12 MUFFINS

These prizewinning muffins are regulars at state fair competitions.

¼ cup shortening
1 cup sugar
2 eggs
1 cup milk
2½ cups flour
1 teaspoon baking soda
2 teaspoons cream of tartar
¼ teaspoon salt
1½ cups rinsed and
   drained blueberries

Preheat oven to 350 degrees F. Spray muffin cups with nonstick cooking spray.

In a large bowl, cream shortening and sugar. Add eggs and milk.

Combine flour, baking soda, cream of tartar, and salt in another bowl. Add to creamed mixture just until moistened. Fold in blueberries.

Fill muffin cups ⅔ full. Bake for 20–25 minutes. Cool for 5 minutes and remove from pan.

· CRUNCHY APPLE ·

This apple muffin recipe makes great muffin tops.

1 cup sugar
½ cup canola oil
2 eggs
1 teaspoon vanilla
1 ½ cups flour
1 teaspoon baking soda
½ teaspoon apple pie spice
2 cups grated apples
½ cup chopped walnuts, optional
½ cup raisins, optional

Crunch topping
¼ cup butter
½ cup flour
3 tablespoons sugar

Preheat oven to 350 degrees F. Spray muffin cups with nonstick cooking spray.

Cream sugar, oil, eggs, and vanilla in small bowl.

Mix together flour, baking soda, and apple pie spice in large bowl. Add creamed mixture, stirring just until moistened. Fold in apples and nuts and raisins if using.

Fill muffin cups ⅔ full.

For the crunch topping, mix butter, flour, and sugar with a fork or pastry blender in small bowl. Spoon evenly over batter in muffin cups.

Bake for 25–30 minutes. Cool for 5 minutes and remove from pan.

· SPICY PEACH & NUT ·

MAKES 18 MUFFINS

Apricots can be substituted for peaches in this
delightfully light-textured muffin.

1 can (15 ounces) peaches, drained
  and chopped; reserve juice
Buttermilk
2½ cups flour
1 ½ cups sugar
1 teaspoon baking powder
1 ½ teaspoons baking soda
½ teaspoon nutmeg
½ teaspoon cloves
½ teaspoon ginger
1 teaspoon cinnamon
3 tablespoons butter,
  melted and cooled
2 eggs

Glaze
4 tablespoons reserved
  peach juice
1 cup powdered sugar
½ cup chopped walnuts

Preheat oven to 350 degrees F. Spray muffin cups with nonstick cooking spray.

Measure 4 tablespoons reserved peach juice into small bowl and set aside. Add buttermilk to remaining reserved peach juice to equal 1 cup.

Combine flour, sugar, baking powder, baking soda, nutmeg, cloves, ginger, and cinnamon in large bowl.

In medium bowl, combine butter and eggs. Stir in buttermilk mixture. Fold peaches into egg mixture. Mix egg mixture with dry ingredients just until moistened.

Fill muffin cups ⅔ full. Bake for 20–25 minutes.

For the glaze, mix together reserved peach juice, powdered sugar, and nuts. Spread glaze evenly over warm muffins and serve.

· BLUEBERRY OATMEAL ·

Oats make this muffin more textured, spices make it more
flavorful, and buttermilk takes it up a notch from good to great.

1 cup firmly packed
  light brown sugar
¼ cup unsalted butter
1 egg
1 ⅛ cups quick oats
1 cup buttermilk
1 tablespoon vanilla
1 ¼ cups flour
1 tablespoon baking powder
1 teaspoon salt
1 teaspoon cinnamon
½ teaspoon baking soda
½ teaspoon nutmeg
½ cup finely chopped walnuts
1 ⅓ cups fresh blueberries

Preheat oven to 400 degrees F. Spray muffin cups with nonstick cooking spray.

In large bowl, cream brown sugar and butter. Add egg and beat well. Stir in oats, buttermilk, and vanilla.

In another large bowl, mix flour, baking powder, salt, cinnamon, baking soda, nutmeg, and walnuts together. Add butter mixture, stirring just until moistened. Fold in blueberries.

Fill muffin cups ⅔ full. Bake for 15–20 minutes. Cool for 5 minutes and remove from pan.

· APPLE-RAISIN OATMEAL ·

MAKES 12 MUFFINS

These muffins are coarsely textured but very tasty.

1 egg
¾ cup milk
1 cup raisins
1 chopped apple
½ cup canola oil
1 cup whole-wheat flour
1 cup quick oats
¼ cup sugar
2 teaspoons baking powder
1 teaspoon salt
1 teaspoon nutmeg
2 teaspoons cinnamon

Preheat oven to 400 degrees F. Spray muffin cups with nonstick cooking spray.

In large bowl, beat egg and stir in milk, raisins, apple, and oil.

In another bowl, combine flour, oats, sugar, baking powder, salt, nutmeg, and cinnamon. Add dry ingredients to egg mixture and stir until just moistened.

Fill muffin cups ¾ full. Bake for 15–20 minutes. Cool for 5 minutes and remove from pan.

· TANGY LEMON ·

MAKES 12 MUFFINS

These muffins are reminiscent of tangy lemon squares.

1¾ cups flour
¾ cup sugar
1 tablespoon lemon zest
1 teaspoon baking powder
¾ teaspoon baking soda
¼ teaspoon salt
1 container (8 ounces)
  lemon yogurt
6 tablespoons butter,
  melted and cooled
1 egg, room temperature
1 tablespoon fresh lemon juice

Glaze
⅓ cup fresh lemon juice
¼ cup sugar
2 teaspoons lemon zest

Preheat oven to 400 degrees F. Spray muffin cups with nonstick cooking spray.

In large bowl, mix flour, sugar, lemon zest, baking powder, baking soda, and salt together; then make well in center.

Whisk yogurt, butter, egg, and lemon juice in another bowl. Stir egg mixture into dry ingredients just until moistened.

Fill muffin cups ¾ full. Bake for 20 minutes.

Meanwhile, to make the glaze, cook lemon juice, sugar, and lemon zest in a nonaluminum saucepan over low heat until sugar dissolves.

Pierce each muffin 6–8 times with toothpick. Drizzle hot glaze over each muffin. Serve at room temperature.

· RUM RAISIN ·

Even if you're not fond of rum, you'll love these muffins.
Soaking the raisins and currants in real rum makes all the difference.

½ cup golden raisins
½ cup dried currants
½ cup dark rum or 2 tablespoons
    rum extract plus ¼ cup water
2 cups flour
¾ cup sugar
1 ½ teaspoons baking powder
½ teaspoon baking soda
¼ teaspoon salt
¼ teaspoon freshly
    ground nutmeg
6 tablespoons butter, softened
1 cup sour cream
1 egg, room temperature
¾ teaspoon vanilla

Glaze
⅓ cup powdered sugar
Several drops fresh lemon juice

In small bowl, cover raisins and currants in rum and soak overnight, stirring occasionally.

Preheat oven to 400 degrees F. Spray muffin cups with nonstick cooking spray. Drain fruit, reserving rum.

Mix flour, sugar, baking powder, baking soda, salt, and nutmeg in large bowl. Cut in butter until a coarse meal forms. Mix in fruit.

In small bowl, whisk sour cream, egg, vanilla, and 2 tablespoons reserved rum until smooth. Stir into flour mixture just until moistened. Fill muffin cups ¾ full. Bake for 15–20 minutes. Cool for 5 minutes and remove from pan.

To make a thin glaze, combine powdered sugar and lemon juice together with about 1 tablespoon of reserved rum. Drizzle glaze over slightly cooled muffins.

· APPLE & CARROT ·

MAKES 16 MUFFINS

The Granny Smith apples provide a nice tartness and
an attractive color combination with the carrots.

2 eggs
¾ cup sugar
¼ cup canola oil
½ cup buttermilk or milk
2 cups chopped Granny
   Smith apples
½ cup grated carrots
2 cups flour
2 teaspoons baking powder
½ teaspoon baking soda
1 teaspoon cinnamon
½ teaspoon salt

Preheat oven to 350 degrees F. Spray muffin cups with nonstick cooking spray.

Combine eggs, sugar, oil, and buttermilk in large bowl. Stir in apples and carrots.

Mix flour, baking powder, baking soda, cinnamon, and salt together in another bowl. Combine with egg mixture, stirring just until moistened.

Fill muffin cups ⅔ full. Bake for 20–25 minutes. Cool for 5 minutes and remove from pan.

· SPICY APPLE ·

MAKES 12 MUFFINS

This muffin has a gentle taste of spice cake that is enhanced when served with a tablespoon of fruit preserves or apple butter.

1 2/3 cups flour
3 tablespoons sugar
2 1/2 teaspoons baking powder
1 teaspoon cinnamon
1/2 teaspoon nutmeg
1/4 teaspoon salt
1 egg, beaten
1 cup skim milk
2 tablespoons canola oil
1 cup finely chopped
   apple, of choice

Preheat oven to 400 degrees F. Spray muffin cups with nonstick cooking spray.

Combine flour, sugar, baking powder, cinnamon, nutmeg, and salt in large bowl. Make a well in the center of the mixture.

In small bowl, combine egg, milk, and oil. Pour into center of dry ingredients, stirring just until moistened. Fold in apple.

Fill muffin cups 3/4 full. Bake for 15–20 minutes. Cool for 5 minutes and remove from pan.

· CHOCOLATE CHIP-BANANA ·

These muffins capture the flavor of chocolate-covered bananas.

½ cup butter, softened
1 cup firmly packed
　 light brown sugar
2 eggs, lightly beaten
5 to 6 ripe bananas, mashed
2 cups flour
½ teaspoon salt
½ teaspoon baking powder
¾ teaspoon baking soda
¾ cup chopped nuts, of choice
¾ cup mini chocolate chips

Preheat oven to 350 degrees F. Spray muffin cups with nonstick cooking spray.

In large bowl, cream together butter and brown sugar. Add eggs and bananas and mix well.

In another bowl, combine flour with salt, baking powder, and baking soda. Stir in creamed mixture just until moistened. Fold in nuts and chocolate chips.

Fill muffin cups ⅔ full. Bake for 20–25 minutes or until golden brown. Cool for 5 minutes and remove from pan.

· GRAHAM & PEAR ·

MAKES 24 MUFFINS

Graham crackers add a flavorful twist to a muffin
already filled with tasty surprises.

2 cans (16 ounces each) pears
½ cup graham cracker crumbs
4½ cups flour
1 cup firmly packed brown sugar
4 teaspoons baking powder
1 teaspoon salt
2 teaspoons cinnamon
1 teaspoon baking soda
¾ teaspoon ground allspice
1 cup butter or margarine
2 cups light sour cream
4 large eggs
⅔ cup sliced almonds

Streusel topping
4 tablespoons flour
¼ cup firmly packed brown sugar
2 tablespoons graham
   cracker crumbs
½ teaspoon cinnamon
2 tablespoons butter or
   margarine, softened

Preheat oven to 350 degrees F. Spray muffin cups with nonstick cooking spray.

Drain pears and pat dry with paper towels. Chop coarsely and set aside.

In large bowl, stir graham cracker crumbs, flour, brown sugar, baking powder, salt, cinnamon, baking soda, and allspice until well mixed. Cut in butter until crumbly.

In medium bowl, whisk sour cream and eggs. Fold egg mixture, pears, and almonds into dry ingredients. Fill muffin cups ¾ full.

To make the streusel topping, mix flour, brown sugar, graham cracker crumbs and cinnamon in small bowl. Cut in butter to form crumbles and sprinkle evenly over batter in muffin cups. Bake for 25–30 minutes. Cool for 5 minutes and remove from pan.

· APPLE SURPRISE ·

MAKES 12 MUFFINS

Try mixing the ingredients all together for a yummy taste—
like a chocolate-covered apple from the candy store.

2 medium apples, peeled,
   cored, and diced
½ teaspoon cinnamon
1 tablespoon sugar plus ½
   cup sugar, divided
¼ cup chopped nuts, of choice
¼ cup melted butter
¼ cup unsweetened cocoa
¾ cup applesauce
1 ¼ cups flour
¾ teaspoon baking soda
¼ teaspoon salt
1 egg, slightly beaten

Preheat oven to 375 degrees F. Spray muffin cups with nonstick cooking spray.

Combine apples, cinnamon, 1 tablespoon sugar, and nuts in small bowl. Mix well and set aside.

Thoroughly combine butter and cocoa then add applesauce in another bowl.

In large bowl, combine flour, ½ cup sugar, baking soda, and salt. Stir in cocoa mixture and egg just until moistened.

Place 1 tablespoon batter in each of 12 muffin cups then spoon 1 heaping tablespoon apple mixture into each cup, pressing into batter. Cover each cup with 1 tablespoon batter.

Bake for 15–20 minutes. Cool for 5 minutes and remove from pan.

· HONEY-OAT APPLE ·

MAKES 12 MUFFINS

Wheat germ makes this muffin a healthier
treat for a midmorning pick-me-up.

¾ cup milk
1 egg
¼ cup canola oil
¼ cup honey
1 cup rolled oats
1 cup whole-wheat flour
⅓ cup wheat germ
¼ cup firmly packed brown sugar
1 tablespoon baking powder
¾ teaspoon cinnamon
¼ teaspoon salt
½ cup chopped apple, of choice

Preheat oven to 400 degrees F. Spray muffin cups with nonstick cooking spray.

In large bowl, mix milk, egg, oil, and honey thoroughly.

In another bowl, combine oats, flour, wheat germ, brown sugar, baking powder, cinnamon, and salt. Fold in apple. Add to wet ingredients, mixing just until moistened.

Fill muffin cups ⅔ full. Bake for 15–20 minutes. Cool for 5 minutes and remove from pan.

· BLACKBERRY ·

MAKES 24 MUFFINS

What can you say except, "Give me another one, please!"
Those big blackberries are irresistible.

½ cup butter
1 container (6 ounces)
   blackberry yogurt
½ cup sugar
2 eggs
3½ cups flour, divided
2 teaspoons baking powder
1 teaspoon baking soda
½ teaspoon salt
1 cup buttermilk
½ cup skim milk
1 teaspoon vanilla
1 package (16 ounces) frozen
   blackberries, thawed

Topping
½ cup sliced almonds
2 to 3 tablespoons buttermilk
¼ cup sugar
Pinch of cinnamon

Preheat oven to 400 degrees F. Spray muffin cups with nonstick cooking spray.

In large bowl, cream butter with yogurt, sugar, and eggs. In another bowl, combine all but 3 tablespoons flour with baking powder, baking soda, and salt.

Combine milks and vanilla in small bowl. Alternately add milk and flour mixtures to egg mixture.

In large bowl, sprinkle reserved flour over berries and gently fold into batter. Fill each muffin cup ¾ full.

For topping, combine almonds, buttermilk, sugar, and cinnamon and spoon evenly over batter. Bake 15–20 minutes. Cool for 5 minutes and remove from pan.

Note Best when served warm. Refrigerate or freeze leftover muffins. They ferment quickly.

· MINIATURE ORANGE ·

MAKES ABOUT 36 MINIATURE MUFFINS

Make these miniatures for a great addition to any brunch menu.
These bite-size morsels are easy for children to hold and eat.

2 cups sugar, divided
½ cup orange juice
½ cup butter, softened
2 cups flour
1 teaspoon baking soda
1 teaspoon salt
1 cup sour cream
1 teaspoon orange zest
½ cup raisins
½ cup chopped nuts, of choice

Preheat oven to 375 degrees F. Spray miniature muffin cups with nonstick cooking spray.

In small bowl, mix 1 cup sugar and orange juice. Set aside for dipping after muffins are baked.

In large bowl, cream butter and 1 cup sugar.

In medium bowl, combine flour, baking soda, and salt. Add sour cream alternately with dry ingredients to butter mixture until just moistened. Fold in orange zest, raisins, and nuts. The batter will be stiff.

Fill muffins cups ¾ full. Bake for 10–12 minutes. Cool for 5 minutes and remove from pan.

While still warm, dip muffins in orange juice mixture.

· GINGER-ORANGE ·

Aah, the soothing taste of ginger is good for the mind and soul.

¾ cup flour
¾ cup whole-wheat flour
⅔ cup sugar
1 ¼ teaspoons ground ginger
2 teaspoons baking powder
½ teaspoon baking soda
¼ teaspoon salt
1 tablespoon orange zest
7 tablespoons butter, melted
    and cooled to lukewarm
⅓ cup sour cream
⅓ cup fresh orange juice
2 eggs, room temperature

Preheat oven to 400 degrees F. Spray muffin cups with nonstick cooking spray.

Mix flours, sugar, ginger, baking powder, baking soda, and salt in large bowl. Stir in orange zest.

Whisk butter, sour cream, orange juice, and eggs in medium bowl.

Make a well in the center of dry ingredients. Add butter mixture and stir until just blended. The batter will be lumpy.

Fill muffin cups ¾ full. Bake for 15–20 minutes. Cool for 5 minutes and remove from pan.

· ORANGE BLOSSOM ·

The spicy crumb topping is the blossom on the top.

¼ cup sugar
1 tablespoon flour
½ teaspoon cinnamon
¼ teaspoon nutmeg
1 tablespoon butter or margarine
1 egg, slightly beaten
½ cup orange juice
½ cup orange marmalade
2 cups prepared biscuit mix
¼ cup chopped pecans

Preheat oven to 400 degrees F. Spray muffin cups with nonstick cooking spray.

In small bowl, combine sugar, flour, cinnamon, and nutmeg. Cut in butter until crumbly. Set aside.

Combine egg, juice, and marmalade in medium bowl. Add biscuit mix. Stir vigorously for 30 seconds. Stir in nuts.

Fill muffin cups ½ full. Sprinkle crumbly mixture over batter. Bake for 15–20 minutes. Cool for 5 minutes and remove from pan.

· RHUBARB ·

MAKES 12 MUFFINS

These muffins are another favorite of Cyndi's.
Don't limit the use of rhubarb to spring, it is available
in the grocer's frozen-food section all year long.

1 ½ cups firmly packed
   brown sugar
½ cup canola oil
1 egg
1 teaspoon vanilla
1 cup buttermilk
½ cup chopped walnuts
   or pecans
2 ½ cups flour
1 teaspoon baking soda
1 teaspoon baking powder
½ teaspoon salt
1 ½ cups diced rhubarb
Sugar, for sprinkling

Preheat oven to 350 degrees F. Spray muffin cups with nonstick cooking spray.

In large bowl, mix together brown sugar, oil, egg, and vanilla until well blended.

Add buttermilk, nuts, flour, baking soda, baking powder, and salt and mix until moistened. Fold in rhubarb.

Fill muffin cups 2/3 full. Sprinkle a pinch or two of sugar on top of batter.

Bake for 20–25 minutes. Cool for 5 minutes and remove from pan.

· BUTTERMILK & APPLE ·

Rhubarb can be substituted for the apple in this recipe.

¾ cup firmly packed brown sugar
⅓ cup canola oil
1 egg, slightly beaten
1 teaspoon vanilla
1 ½ cups flour
½ teaspoon baking soda
¼ teaspoon salt
1 cup peeled and chopped
   apple, of choice
½ cup buttermilk

Topping
¼ cup firmly packed brown sugar
¼ cup chopped pecans
½ teaspoon cinnamon

Preheat oven to 325 degrees F. Spray muffin cups with nonstick cooking spray.

Blend brown sugar, oil, egg, and vanilla in large bowl.

In medium bowl, combine flour, baking soda, and salt. Add to wet mixture. Stir in apple and buttermilk, and mix just to moisten.

Fill muffin cups ⅔ full.

For the topping, combine brown sugar, pecans, and cinnamon in small bowl. Sprinkle evenly over batter in muffin cups.

Bake for 20–25 minutes. Cool for 5 minutes and remove from pan.

· BANANA STREUSEL ·

If you like bananas, you'll love these muffins. This recipe is
one of Cyndi's favorites to make into a loaf of bread.

2 cups flour
¼ cup sugar
¼ cup firmly packed brown sugar
2 teaspoons baking powder
½ teaspoon baking soda
½ teaspoon salt
½ teaspoon cinnamon
¼ teaspoon nutmeg
3 ripe bananas, mashed
½ cup buttermilk
⅓ cup canola oil
1 egg
¼ cup chopped pecans, optional

Streusel topping
3 tablespoons butter
½ cup flour
3 tablespoons sugar

Preheat oven to 375 degrees F. Spray muffin cups with nonstick cooking spray.

In large mixing bowl, combine flour, sugars, baking powder, baking soda, salt, cinnamon, and nutmeg.

In another bowl, combine bananas, buttermilk, oil, egg, and pecans if using. Stir into flour mixture until just moistened.

Fill muffin cups ⅔ full.

For streusel topping, cut butter into flour and sugar in small bowl. Sprinkle mixture over the batter in the muffin cups.

Bake for 15–20 minutes. Cool for 5 minutes and remove from pan.

· PINEAPPLE & COCONUT ·

MAKES 24 MUFFINS

The full creamy flavor of piña colada can be enjoyed
in these beautifully light-textured muffins.

1 box yellow cake mix
1 cup water
¼ cup butter, melted and cooled
2 eggs, beaten
1 can (8 ounces) crushed
   pineapple, drained, reserving
   3 tablespoons juice
⅔ cup flaked coconut

Topping
⅓ cup flaked coconut
3 tablespoons pineapple juice
¾ cup powdered sugar

Preheat oven to 350 degrees F. Spray
muffin cups with nonstick cooking spray.

In large bowl, combine cake mix, water,
butter, eggs, pineapple, and coconut.
Mix thoroughly, but do not beat.

Fill muffin cups ¾ full. Bake for
25–30 minutes. Remove muffins
from oven and turn oven to broil.

To make topping, mix coconut,
pineapple juice, and powdered sugar
in small bowl. Spoon mixture evenly
over hot muffins.

Broil 1–2 minutes just until coconut
topping is slightly bubbly. Cool for
5 minutes and remove from pan.

· ORANGE CRUNCH ·

MAKES 14 TO 16 MUFFINS

The cereal nuggets give this muffin its nutty crunch.

2 cups flour
1/3 cup sugar
1 teaspoon baking powder
1/2 teaspoon baking soda
3/4 teaspoon salt
1/2 cup malted cereal nuggets
2 eggs, well beaten
1 tablespoon orange zest
1 cup orange juice
1/3 cup canola oil

Preheat oven to 400 degrees F. Spray muffin cups with nonstick cooking spray.

Combine flour, sugar, baking powder, baking soda, and salt in small bowl.

In large bowl, mix cereal, eggs, orange zest, orange juice, and oil. Add flour mixture and stir just until moistened.

Fill muffin cups 2/3 full. Bake for 15–20 minutes. Cool for 5 minutes and remove from pan.

· TROPICAL FRUIT ·

MAKES 18 MUFFINS

Although passion fruit juice and guava jelly are sometimes difficult to locate, these muffins make the search worth the effort.

1 package dry active yeast
¼ cup very warm (105–115 degrees F) water
½ cup cooked and mashed sweet potato
¼ cup butter, softened
½ cup sugar
¾ teaspoon salt
½ cup warm passion fruit juice
1 egg, beaten
2 cups flour
¼ cup drained crushed pineapple
⅓ cup guava jelly

Preheat oven to 375 degrees F. Spray muffin cups with nonstick cooking spray.

Dissolve yeast in water.

Beat sweet potato and butter in large bowl. Add sugar and salt. Beat 2 minutes. Add passion fruit juice, egg, and yeast mixture. Beat 1 minute. Stir in flour just until moistened. Fold in pineapple.

Fill muffin cups ⅔ full. Let rise just to the tops of the cups, about 45 minutes.

Spoon about 1 teaspoon of guava jelly on the center of each muffin.

Bake for 20 minutes or until golden brown. Cool for 5 minutes and remove from pan.

· CRANBERRY & MAPLE ·

In the summer when fresh cranberries aren't plentiful, use a can
of whole cranberry sauce and reduce the sugar to ½ cup.

2 cups flour
½ cup chopped walnuts
2 teaspoons baking powder
½ teaspoon baking soda
½ teaspoon salt
1 ½ cups sliced or chopped
   cranberries
½ cup unsalted butter, softened
2 eggs
1 cup sugar
⅔ cup buttermilk
2 teaspoons maple flavoring

Preheat oven to 350 degrees F. Spray muffin cups with nonstick cooking spray.

In large bowl, mix flour, walnuts, baking powder, baking soda, and salt. Stir in cranberries.

In another bowl, beat together butter, eggs, sugar, buttermilk, and maple flavoring. Stir into dry ingredients just until moistened.

Fill muffin cups ⅔ full. Bake for 20–25 minutes. Cool for 5 minutes and remove from pan.

· GRANNY'S CRANBERRY ·

MAKES 12 MUFFINS

Use dried or frozen cranberries if fresh cranberries are not available.

¾ cup halved cranberries
½ cup powdered sugar
2 cups flour
3 teaspoons baking powder
½ teaspoon salt
¼ cup sugar
1 egg, well beaten
1 cup milk
4 tablespoons shortening, melted

Preheat oven to 375 degrees F. Spray muffin cups with nonstick cooking spray.

In small bowl, mix cranberries with powdered sugar.

In large bowl, combine flour, baking powder, salt, and sugar. Stir in egg, milk, and shortening all at once. Fold in cranberries.

Fill muffin cups ⅔ full. Bake for 20–25 minutes. Cool for 5 minutes and remove from pan.

· RASPBERRY ·

MAKES 12 MUFFINS

Try these muffins as a loaf cake. Bake at 350 degrees F for 1 hour
or until wooden toothpick inserted in center comes out clean.

1 ½ cups flour
½ teaspoon baking soda
½ teaspoon salt
1 ½ teaspoons cinnamon
1 cup sugar
2 eggs, well beaten
⅔ cup canola oil
1 package (12 ounces)
   frozen unsweetened
   raspberries, thawed
½ cup chopped pecans

Preheat oven to 400 degrees F. Spray muffin cups with nonstick cooking spray.

In medium bowl, mix flour, baking soda, salt, cinnamon, and sugar. Make a well in the center and stir in eggs and oil. Fold in undrained raspberries and pecans.

Fill muffin cups ⅔ full. Bake for 15–20 minutes. Cool for 5 minutes and remove from pan.

· RASPBERRY WINE ·

MAKES 16 TO 18 MUFFINS

Raspberry wine isn't a staple in most kitchens,
so substitute a raspberry-cranberry juice cocktail.

3 cups flour, divided
1 tablespoon baking powder
½ teaspoon salt
⅛ teaspoon baking soda
½ cup butter or margarine
1 cup sugar
1 teaspoon vanilla
2 eggs
½ cup raspberry wine
½ cup water
1 cup coarsely chopped fresh
  or frozen raspberries

Preheat oven to 400 degrees F. Spray muffin cups with nonstick cooking spray.

Reserve 3 tablespoons flour in small bowl.

In large bowl, stir together remaining flour, baking powder, salt, and baking soda. Set aside.

In another bowl, beat butter. Add sugar and vanilla, beating until smooth. Add eggs, 1 at a time, beating well.

Stir together wine and water. Add wine mixture and creamed mixture to flour mixture, stirring just until moistened. Toss together reserved flour and berries and gently fold into batter.

Fill muffin cups ⅔ full. Bake for 18–20 minutes. Cool for 5 minutes and remove from pan.

· CHEERY CHERRY ·

MAKES 12 MUFFINS

For a different cherry flavor, substitute chopped fresh cherries
or dried cherries. Cherry lovers won't stop at just one muffin.

2 cups flour
1/3 cup sugar
1/3 cup quartered
  maraschino cherries
1 tablespoon baking powder
1/2 teaspoon salt
3/4 cup buttermilk
1/4 cup canola oil
4 tablespoons cherry juice
1 egg, beaten
1 teaspoon almond extract

Topping
4 tablespoons finely
  chopped almonds
3 tablespoons sugar

Preheat oven to 350 degrees F. Spray muffin cups with nonstick cooking spray.

In large mixing bowl, combine flour, sugar, cherries, baking powder, and salt.

In another bowl, mix buttermilk, oil, cherry juice, egg, and almond extract.

Make a well in dry ingredients and stir in liquid just to moisten.

Fill muffin cups 2/3 full.

For the topping, combine almonds and sugar, and sprinkle over batter. Bake for 20–25 minutes.

Note Cool 10 minutes before removing from muffin cups.

· FROSTED PUMPKIN ·

MAKES 16 MUFFINS

This recipe is a fall favorite that can be enjoyed all year long, thanks to canned pumpkin. These muffins taste like our favorite pumpkin bars.

1 cup flour
½ cup sugar
2 teaspoons baking powder
½ teaspoon cinnamon
½ teaspoon nutmeg
¼ teaspoon salt
¼ cup butter or margarine
1 egg, beaten
½ cup canned pumpkin
½ cup evaporated milk
½ cup raisins

Cream cheese frosting
3 ounces cream cheese,
   at room temperature
½ cup butter or margarine
2 tablespoons milk
1 teaspoon vanilla
2 cups powdered sugar

Preheat oven to 400 degrees F. Spray muffin cups with nonstick cooking spray.

Combine flour, sugar, baking powder, cinnamon, nutmeg, and salt together in medium bowl. Cut in butter until mixture resembles cornmeal.

In small bowl, combine egg with pumpkin and milk. Stir in raisins. Add egg mixture to dry ingredients, stirring just to moisten.

Fill muffin cups ⅔ full. Bake for 15–20 minutes. Cool for 5 minutes and remove from pan. Completely cool before frosting.

In large bowl, beat cream cheese, butter, milk, vanilla, and powdered sugar until smooth. Frost cooled muffins.

· RICH COFFEE-DATE ·

MAKES 12 MUFFINS

Break time is extra special when serving these muffins with hot chocolate. The combination creates a delightful mocha taste.

1¾ cups flour
2½ teaspoons baking powder
1 cup water
1 egg
⅓ cup canola oil
¼ cup sugar
1½ teaspoons instant coffee
 powder (not freeze-dried)
¾ teaspoon salt
1 package (8 ounces) pitted dates

Preheat oven to 400 degrees F. Spray muffin cups with nonstick cooking spray.

Mix flour and baking powder together in large bowl.

Using a blender, mix water, egg, oil, sugar, instant coffee powder, salt, and dates until dates are coarsely chopped. Pour date mixture over dry ingredients, stirring just until moistened.

Fill muffin cups ⅔ full. Bake for 15–20 minutes. Cool for 5 minutes and remove from pan.

vegetable

· ZUCCHINI-NUT ·

Put those extra zucchinis to good use in these muffins,
and freeze to enjoy in the off-season.

2 eggs, slightly beaten
½ cup firmly packed brown sugar
½ cup honey
½ cup butter or
    margarine, melted
1 teaspoon vanilla
1¾ cups flour
1 teaspoon baking soda
1 teaspoon salt
½ teaspoon baking powder
½ teaspoon nutmeg
1 ½ teaspoons cinnamon
1 cup granola cereal
½ cup chopped walnuts
2 cups grated zucchini

Preheat oven to 350 degrees F. Spray muffin cups with nonstick cooking spray.

In large bowl, beat eggs, brown sugar, honey, butter, and vanilla.

In another bowl, stir together flour, baking soda, salt, baking powder, nutmeg, and cinnamon.

Add dry ingredients to egg mixture, stirring just until moistened. Fold in granola, nuts, and zucchini.

Fill muffin cups ¾ full. Bake for 20–25 minutes. Cool for 5 minutes and remove from pan.

· ZUCCHINI-OATMEAL ·

The oatmeal and pecans give these muffins a nutty flavor.

2½ cups flour
1½ cups sugar
1 cup chopped pecans
½ cup uncooked quick oats
1 tablespoon baking powder
1 teaspoon salt
1 teaspoon cinnamon
4 eggs, slightly beaten
1 medium zucchini, grated,
   drained, and liquid
   squeezed out
¾ cup canola oil

Preheat oven to 400 degrees F. Spray miniature muffin cups with nonstick cooking spray.

In large bowl, combine flour, sugar, pecans, oats, baking powder, salt, and cinnamon. Mix in eggs, zucchini, and oil just until moistened.

Fill muffin cups ⅔ full. Bake for 10–15 minutes. Cool for 5 minutes and remove from pan.

· MUSHROOM ·

MAKES 12 TO 16 MUFFINS

For those who love mushrooms, this muffin is best
when served warm with a salad or bowl of soup.

1 can (4 ounces) mushrooms,
stems and pieces, or 1 cup
fresh, sliced mushrooms
and increase milk to 1 cup
1 tablespoon butter
2 cups flour
¼ cup sugar
3 teaspoons baking powder
1 teaspoon salt
1 egg
¾ cup milk
½ cup shredded white
cheddar cheese
¼ cup canola oil

Preheat oven to 400 degrees F. Spray
muffin cups with nonstick cooking spray.

Drain mushrooms, reserving ¼ cup
liquid. Sauté mushrooms in butter in
a small skillet.

In large bowl, combine flour, sugar,
baking powder, and salt.

In small bowl, beat egg slightly with a
fork and stir in mushroom liquid and
milk. Stir in cheese, mushrooms, and
oil. Add to dry ingredients and stir just
until moistened.

Fill muffin cups ⅔ full. Bake for
15–20 minutes. Cool for 5 minutes
and remove from pan.

· SWEET POTATO ·

Fragrant with spices, these muffins spark appetites
for a hearty breakfast or dinner.

1 ½ cups flour
¼ cup firmly packed
   light brown sugar
1 tablespoon baking powder
½ teaspoon salt
½ teaspoon cinnamon
¼ teaspoon nutmeg
1 egg
½ cup milk
1 cup cooked and mashed
   sweet potatoes
¼ cup butter, melted
½ cup raisins

Heat oven to 400 degrees F. Spray muffin cups with nonstick cooking spray.

In medium bowl, combine flour, brown sugar, baking powder, salt, cinnamon, and nutmeg.

In small bowl, beat together egg, milk, sweet potatoes, and butter. Add egg mixture to dry ingredients, stirring just until moistened. Fold in raisins.

Fill muffin cups ⅔ full. Bake for 15–20 minutes. Cool for 5 minutes and remove from pan.

· RED & GREEN BELL PEPPER ·

MAKES 10 MUFFINS

This is a great-smelling complement to hearty soups.

½ cup butter
⅓ cup chopped green onions
⅓ cup finely chopped
   red bell pepper
¼ cup finely chopped
   green bell pepper
⅔ cup sour cream
2 eggs
1 ½ cups flour
2 tablespoons sugar
2 teaspoons baking powder
¾ teaspoon salt
½ teaspoon baking soda
½ teaspoon dried basil
¼ teaspoon dried tarragon

Preheat oven to 400 degrees F. Spray muffin cups with nonstick cooking spray.

Melt butter in skillet with onions and peppers and cook until tender, about 7 minutes, stirring often. Cool to lukewarm.

Whisk sour cream and eggs in medium bowl. Stir in cooled onion mixture.

Combine flour, sugar, baking powder, salt, baking soda, basil, and tarragon in large bowl and make well in the center. Add sour cream mixture, stirring just until blended.

Fill muffin cups ¾ full. Bake for 15–20 minutes. Cool for 5 minutes and remove from pan.

· CREAMY CORN ·

MAKES 12 MUFFINS

This is a true corny corn muffin for whole-wheat lovers.

1 cup whole-wheat flour
1 cup yellow cornmeal
4 teaspoons baking powder
½ teaspoon salt
¼ cup sugar
2 eggs, slightly beaten
1 cup skim milk
2 tablespoons butter or
    margarine, melted
1 cup cream-style corn

Preheat oven to 400 degrees F. Spray muffin cups with nonstick cooking spray.

Combine flour, cornmeal, baking powder, salt, and sugar in large bowl.

In another bowl, beat together eggs, milk, butter, and corn. Add egg mixture to flour mixture, stirring just until moistened.

Fill muffin cups ⅔ full. Bake for 15–20 minutes. Cool for 5 minutes and remove from pan.

· CORNBREAD ·

Heat the muffin tin before filling cups with batter for perfect browning.

1 cup yellow cornmeal
1 cup flour
3 tablespoons sugar
Pinch of salt
4 teaspoons baking powder
4 tablespoons butter, melted
1 cup milk
1 egg, slightly beaten

Preheat oven to 400 degrees F. Spray muffin cups with nonstick cooking spray.

In large bowl, mix together cornmeal, flour, sugar, salt, and baking powder. Add butter, milk, and egg, stirring until moistened.

Fill muffin cups ¾ full. Bake for 10–12 minutes. Cool for 5 minutes and remove from pan.

· JALAPEÑO & CORN ·

MAKES 12 MUFFINS

This one is great with lots of butter. For a twist, mix the jalapeño jelly into the batter—it makes a totally different muffin.

1 cup flour
1 cup yellow cornmeal
¼ cup sugar
1 tablespoon baking powder
½ teaspoon salt
1 teaspoon crushed red
   pepper flakes
1 egg
½ cup plus 1 teaspoon milk
¼ cup corn oil
½ cup shredded cheddar cheese
1 can (17 ounces) cream-style corn
¼ cup mild jalapeño pepper jelly

Preheat oven to 375 degrees F. Spray muffin cups with nonstick cooking spray.

In large bowl, mix together flour, cornmeal, sugar, baking powder, salt, and red pepper flakes.

Whisk together egg, milk, oil, cheese, and corn in small bowl. Pour liquid mixture over dry ingredients, stirring just until moistened.

Fill muffin cups ½ full. Reserve ⅓ batter. With the back of a teaspoon, make a small depression in center of each muffin and drop in 1 teaspoon jalapeño jelly. Spoon reserved batter evenly over jelly.

Bake for 15–20 minutes. Cool for 5 minutes and remove from pan.

· BACON, CHIVE & CORN ·

MAKES 12 MUFFINS

These muffins make a tasty addition to a hot bowl of bean soup on a cold winter night, and they are a true "Queen of Easy" recipe!

1 package (14 ounces)
   corn muffin mix
2 teaspoons snipped chives
Pinch of black pepper
6 slices bacon, crisp-cooked,
   drained, and crumbled

Preheat oven to 400 degrees F. Spray muffin cups with nonstick cooking spray.

Prepare muffin mix according to package directions in large bowl. Fold in chives, pepper, and bacon.

Fill muffin cup 2/3 full. Bake for 15–17 minutes. Cool for 5 minutes and remove from pan.

· QUICK CORN ·

MAKES 10–12 MUFFINS

The cheesy taste highlights this quick and easy corn muffin recipe.

1 package (14 ounces)
   corn muffin mix
1 can (8.75 ounces)
   cream-style corn
1 egg, slightly beaten
½ cup shredded American cheese
Dash of hot pepper sauce

Preheat oven to 400 degrees F. Spray muffin cups with nonstick cooking spray.

Combine muffin mix, corn, egg, cheese, and pepper sauce in large bowl, mixing just until blended.

Fill muffin cups ⅔ full. Bake for 12–15 minutes. Cool for 5 minutes and remove from pan.

favorites

· P. B. & J. ·

Jelly and peanuts top off this muffin, giving it an extra peanutty flavor.

2 cups flour
1/2 cup sugar
2 1/2 teaspoons baking powder
1/2 teaspoon salt
1/2 cup chunky peanut butter
2 tablespoons butter
   or margarine
1 cup milk
2 eggs, well beaten
1/4 cup currant jelly, or jelly
   of choice, melted
1/2 cup finely chopped peanuts

Preheat oven to 400 degrees F. Spray muffin cups with nonstick cooking spray.

Combine flour, sugar, baking powder, and salt in large bowl. Cut in peanut butter and butter until mixture resembles coarse crumbs. Add milk and eggs all at once, stirring just until moistened.

Fill muffin cups 2/3 full. Bake for 15–17 minutes. Cool for 5 minutes and remove from pan.

Immediately brush with melted jelly and dip in chopped peanuts.

· BREAKFAST ·

These muffins have the spicy and sugary taste of doughnuts.
Use miniature muffin pans for a resemblance to doughnut holes.

1 ½ cups plus 2 tablespoons flour
¾ cup sugar
2 teaspoons baking powder
¼ teaspoon salt
⅔ teaspoon nutmeg
½ cup milk
1 egg, beaten
⅔ cup butter, melted and divided

Topping
½ cup sugar
1 teaspoon cinnamon
½ teaspoon vanilla

Preheat oven to 400 degrees F. Spray muffin cups with nonstick cooking spray.

In large bowl, combine flour, sugar, baking powder, salt, and nutmeg. Add milk, egg, and ⅓ cup melted butter. Mix thoroughly.

Fill muffin cups ½ full. Bake for 20 minutes or until lightly browned.

While muffins bake, mix sugar, cinnamon, and vanilla in small bowl to make topping.

Remove muffins from tin immediately, dip in remaining ⅓ cup melted butter, and roll in topping mixture.

· POUND CAKE ·

MAKES 12 MUFFINS

These muffins are tasty just plain, but they are even tastier served with fresh fruit and cream.

1¾ cups flour
½ teaspoon salt
¾ teaspoon baking soda
¾ cup sugar
½ cup lightly salted
  butter, softened
½ cup sour cream
1 teaspoon vanilla
½ teaspoon lemon juice
2 eggs

Preheat oven to 350 degrees F. Spray muffin cups with nonstick cooking spray.

In small bowl, mix together flour, salt, and baking soda.

In large bowl, beat sugar and butter until fluffy. Beat in sour cream, vanilla, and lemon juice. Beat in eggs, 1 at a time. Stir in dry ingredients just until moistened.

Fill muffin cups ⅔ full. Bake for 20–25 minutes. Cool for 5 minutes and remove from pan.

· POPPY SEED COFFEE CAKE ·

MAKES 30 MUFFINS

These are absolutely delicious and are Georgie's
favorite poppy seed muffins.

¼ cup poppy seeds
1 cup buttermilk
1 teaspoon almond extract
1 cup butter
2 cups sugar, divided
4 eggs, separated
2½ cups flour
1 teaspoon baking powder
1 teaspoon baking soda
1 teaspoon cinnamon

Preheat oven to 350 degrees F. Spray muffin cups with nonstick cooking spray.

In large bowl, combine poppy seeds, buttermilk, and almond extract. Set aside. In small bowl, cream butter and 1 ½ cups sugar. Add egg yolks and beat. Combine buttermilk and creamed mixtures.

In another large bowl, combine flour, baking powder, and baking soda and add to buttermilk mixture just until moistened. In medium bowl, beat egg whites until stiff. Fold into flour mixture. Fill muffin cups ⅓ full.

Mix together ½ cup sugar and cinnamon and sprinkle half of the mixture evenly over batter in muffin cups. Divide remaining batter into muffin cups. Sprinkle remaining sugar-cinnamon mixture over batter. Cut through each cup with knife to create a marbled effect.

Bake for 20–25 minutes. Cool for 5 minutes and remove from pan.

· ORANGE POPPY SEED ·

MAKES 12 MUFFINS

These are delightfully different from other poppy seed
muffins with a hint of orange and nutmeg.

¾ cup sugar
¼ cup butter, softened
½ teaspoon orange zest
2 eggs
2 cups flour
2½ teaspoons baking powder
½ teaspoon salt
¼ teaspoon nutmeg
1 cup milk
¼ cup golden raisins
½ cup chopped pecans
5 tablespoons poppy seeds

Preheat oven to 400 degrees F. Spray
muffin cups with nonstick cooking spray.

In large bowl, cream sugar, butter, and
orange zest. Add eggs, 1 at a time,
beating well after each addition.

Combine flour, baking powder, salt,
and nutmeg in medium bowl. Add to
creamed mixture alternately with milk,
beating well after each addition. Fold
in raisins, nuts, and poppy seeds.

Fill muffin cups ¾ full. Bake for
15–20 minutes, or until lightly browned.
Cool for 5 minutes and remove from pan.

· MAPLE-PECAN ·

MAKES 12 MUFFINS

These wonderfully cake-like muffins are chunky with pecans.

1 ½ cups flour
2 teaspoons baking powder
¼ teaspoon salt
¼ teaspoon allspice
1¾ cups coarsely chopped
   toasted pecans
½ cup firmly packed
   dark brown sugar
½ cup butter, melted
⅓ cup milk
¼ cup maple syrup
1 egg
1 teaspoon vanilla

Preheat oven to 400 degrees F. Generously spray muffin cups with nonstick cooking spray.

Mix flour, baking powder, salt, and allspice in large bowl. Stir in pecans.

Whisk brown sugar, butter, milk, syrup, egg, and vanilla in medium bowl.

Make a well in the center of dry ingredients. Add butter mixture to well and stir into dry ingredients until just moistened.

Fill muffin cups ¾ full. Bake for 15–20 minutes, or until golden brown. Cool for 5 minutes and remove from pan.

· WALNUT STREUSEL ·

MAKES 18 MUFFINS

This muffin gets top honors for texture, appearance,
and flavor. No wonder it is Georgie's favorite.

3 cups flour, divided
1 ½ cups firmly packed
   brown sugar
¾ cup butter or margarine
1 cup chopped walnuts, divided
2 teaspoons baking powder
½ teaspoon nutmeg
½ teaspoon ginger
½ teaspoon baking soda
½ teaspoon salt
1 cup buttermilk or sour milk
2 eggs, beaten

Preheat oven to 350 degrees F. Spray muffin cups with nonstick cooking spray.

In medium bowl, combine 2 cups flour and brown sugar. Cut in butter to make fine crumbs.

In small bowl, combine ¾ cup of the crumbs and ¼ cup of the walnuts. Set aside.

Into remaining crumb mixture, stir in remaining 1 cup of flour, baking powder, nutmeg, ginger, baking soda, salt, and remaining ¾ cup walnuts.

In another small bowl, combine buttermilk and eggs and stir into dry ingredients just to moisten. Fill muffin cups ⅔ full. Top each with a generous spoonful of reserved crumb-nut mixture.

Bake for 20–25 minutes or until springy to the touch. Cool for 5 minutes and remove from pan.

· COFFEE CAKE ·

MAKES 12 MUFFINS

These tasty treats are superb for a coffee break, served warm or cold. As a quick alternative, bake in a 9 x 13-inch baking dish.

2¼ cups flour
1 cup sugar
½ cup butter or
  margarine, melted
1 egg
1 cup buttermilk
1 ½ teaspoons baking soda
½ cup chopped walnuts
  or pecans
½ cup raisins

Preheat oven to 375 degrees F. Spray muffin cups with nonstick cooking spray.

In large bowl, combine flour and sugar. Pour butter over flour mixture, mixing until crumbly. Set aside 1 cup of mixture for topping.

Add egg, buttermilk, baking soda, nuts, and raisins to remainder of flour mixture, stirring just until moistened. Batter will be thin and lumpy.

Fill muffin cups ¾ full. Sprinkle reserved mixture over top of each muffin. Bake for 15–20 minutes. Cool for 5 minutes and remove from pan.

· SPICE CAKE ·

These muffins are a real hit when served with pumpkin mousse.

¼ cup shortening
¼ cup sugar
1 egg
½ cup molasses
1 ½ cups flour
¾ teaspoon baking soda
¼ teaspoon salt
½ teaspoon cinnamon
½ teaspoon ginger
¼ teaspoon cloves
½ cup hot water

Preheat oven to 375 degrees F. Spray muffin cups with nonstick cooking spray.

In large bowl, cream together shortening and sugar. Beat in egg and molasses.

In large bowl, combine flour, baking soda, salt, cinnamon, ginger, and cloves. Stir into molasses mixture. Gradually add hot water, mixing until moistened.

Fill muffin cups ⅔ full. Bake for 15–20 minutes. Cool for 5 minutes and remove from pan.

· SURPRISE ·

You will find a delicious surprise in every bite of these muffins.

2 cups flour
1/4 cup sugar
1 teaspoon baking powder
1/2 teaspoon baking soda
1/4 teaspoon salt
1/4 cup butter, melted
1 cup plain yogurt
1/4 cup milk
1 egg
1/2 teaspoon vanilla
1/4 cup jam or preserves , of choice
Powdered sugar, optional

Preheat oven to 400 degrees F. Spray muffin cups with nonstick cooking spray.

In large bowl, mix flour, sugar, baking powder, baking soda, and salt, stirring until well blended.

Pour butter into another bowl. Add yogurt and milk, stirring until smooth. Beat in egg and vanilla.

Add butter mixture to dry ingredients, stirring just until moistened.

Fill muffin cups 1/2 full. Spoon 1 teaspoon of the jam on the batter in each cup. Top with remaining batter.

Bake for 15–20 minutes. Let stand 5 minutes, remove to a cooling rack, and sift powdered sugar over each muffin before serving, if desired.

· QUICK SESAME & CHEESE ·

MAKES ABOUT 15 MUFFINS

Try mixing toasted sesame seeds into the batter
for a more distinct sesame flavor.

2 tablespoons sesame seeds
½ cup minced onion
2 tablespoons butter
3 cups prepared biscuit mix
1 ½ cups grated sharp
   cheddar cheese, divided
2 eggs, well beaten
1 cup milk

Preheat oven to 400 degrees F. Spray muffin cups with nonstick cooking spray.

Toast sesame seeds in small frying pan over medium heat until lightly browned. Set aside to cool.

In another small frying pan, sauté onion in butter until translucent.

In large bowl, stir biscuit mix and 1 cup cheese together.

In small bowl, combine eggs, milk, and onion. Add to cheese mixture and mix vigorously for 30 seconds.

Fill muffin cups ⅔ full. Sprinkle tops with remaining cheese and the sesame seeds.

Bake for 15–20 minutes. Cool for 5 minutes and remove from pan.

· CHEDDAR RYE ·

MAKES 12 MUFFINS

This is a flavorful, heavy muffin that is very tasty
with potato soup or a sauerkraut dish.

½ cup flour
½ cup rye flour
3 tablespoons sugar
2 teaspoons baking powder
1 teaspoon caraway seeds
½ teaspoon baking soda
½ teaspoon salt
1⅔ cups finely grated extra-
   sharp cheddar cheese
6 tablespoons canola oil
⅔ cup sour cream
½ cup milk
1 egg, room temperature
1 teaspoon Worcestershire sauce

Preheat oven to 400 degrees F. Spray muffin cups with nonstick cooking spray.

Mix flours, sugar, baking powder, caraway seeds, baking soda, and salt in large bowl. Stir cheese into dry ingredients.

Whisk oil, sour cream, milk, egg, and Worcestershire sauce in medium bowl until smooth. Add sour cream mixture to dry ingredients, stirring just until moistened.

Fill muffin cups ¾ full. Bake for 15–20 minutes. Cool for 5 minutes and remove from pan.

· DOUBLE FUDGE ·

MAKES 16 MUFFINS

Like brownies, these muffins are definitely
for the chocolate connoisseurs.

5 ounces coarsely chopped
   semisweet chocolate
2 ounces coarsely chopped
   unsweetened chocolate
1/3 cup butter
3/4 cup sour cream
2/3 cup firmly packed brown sugar
1/4 cup light corn syrup
1 egg
1 1/4 teaspoons vanilla
1 1/2 cups flour
1 teaspoon baking soda
1/4 teaspoon salt
5 ounces semisweet chocolate,
   cut into 1/3-inch pieces or 1 cup
   semisweet chocolate chips

Preheat oven to 400 degrees F. Spray muffin cups with nonstick cooking spray.

Melt chopped chocolates and butter in medium bowl in microwave or in a double boiler. Stir until smooth. Cool slightly. Whisk sour cream, brown sugar, corn syrup, egg, and vanilla into chocolate.

Mix flour, baking soda, and salt in large bowl. Mix in chocolate pieces. Make a well in the center of dry ingredients.

Add chocolate mixture to well and stir into dry ingredients just until just moistened.

Fill muffin cups 3/4 full. Bake for 15–20 minutes. Cool for 5 minutes and remove from pan.

· PIZZA ·

MAKES 12 MUFFINS

This is a muffin of a different flavor. Serve warm with salad or cheese.

2 cups flour
¼ cup grated Parmesan cheese
1 tablespoon sugar
2 teaspoons baking powder
½ teaspoon baking soda
¼ teaspoon cayenne pepper
¼ cup chopped pimiento-stuffed green olives or black olives
¼ cup finely chopped tomato
1 ½ teaspoons Italian seasoning mix
1 medium clove garlic, minced
2 eggs
½ cup olive oil
⅓ cup milk
⅓ cup sour cream

Preheat oven to 400 degrees F. Spray muffin cups with nonstick cooking spray.

Mix flour, cheese, sugar, baking powder, baking soda, and cayenne in large bowl. Stir in olives, tomato, Italian seasoning, and garlic.

In small bowl, whisk eggs, then add oil, milk, and sour cream. Add to flour mixture, stirring just until moistened.

Fill muffin cups ¾ full. Bake for 15–20 minutes or until golden brown. Cool for 5 minutes and remove from pan.

· BACON CORNETTES ·

MAKES 12 MUFFINS

These are excellent cornmeal muffins for the bacon lover.

10 to 12 slices bacon
1 cup flour
¼ cup sugar
4 teaspoons baking powder
¾ teaspoon salt
1 cup yellow cornmeal
2 eggs, well beaten
1 cup milk
¼ cup canola oil

Preheat oven to 425 degrees F. Spray muffin cups with nonstick cooking spray.

Cook bacon until crisp then drain and crumble.

In large bowl, combine flour, sugar, baking powder, and salt; then stir in cornmeal. Add eggs, milk, and oil. Mix just until moistened. Stir in bacon. If desired, save some bacon crumble for the top of the muffins.

Fill muffin cups ⅔ full. Bake for 15–20 minutes. Cool for 5 minutes and remove from pan.

· DILLY ·

MAKES 12 MUFFINS

Cyndi bakes this recipe in a round dish to serve
as a bread on special occasions.

1 packet yeast
¼ cup warm water
1 cup cottage cheese,
   heated to lukewarm
2 tablespoons sugar
1 tablespoon minced onion
1 tablespoon butter, softened
2 teaspoons dill seeds
1 teaspoon salt
¼ teaspoon baking soda
1 egg
2¼ to 2½ cups flour

Heat oven to 350 degrees F. Spray
muffin cups with nonstick cooking spray.

Soften yeast in warm water.

In large bowl, combine cottage cheese,
sugar, onion, butter, dill seeds, salt,
baking soda, egg, and 2¼ cups of
flour. Add yeast mixture. Stir just until
moistened. If batter too sticky, stir in
an additional ¼ cup of flour. Fill muffin
cups ½ full. Let rise for 30 minutes.

Bake for 15–20 minutes. Cool for
5 minutes and remove from pan.

· DIJON & HAM ·

MAKES 12 TO 14 MUFFINS

This is a hearty muffin for a hearty soup.
You will love the mustardy ham flavor.

1⅔ cups flour
⅓ cup white cornmeal
¼ cup sugar
2 teaspoons dry mustard
1 ½ teaspoons baking powder
¾ teaspoon salt
½ teaspoon baking soda
⅛ teaspoon freshly
   ground black pepper
⅛ teaspoon ground cloves
1 ¼ cups finely chopped
   smoked ham
2 eggs
1 cup buttermilk
⅓ cup canola oil
3 tablespoons Dijon mustard

Preheat oven to 400 degrees F. Spray muffin cups with nonstick cooking spray.

Mix flour, cornmeal, sugar, dry mustard, baking powder, salt, baking soda, pepper, and cloves in large bowl. Stir in ham.

Whisk eggs in medium bowl to blend. Whisk buttermilk, oil, and Dijon into eggs.

Make a well in the center of dry ingredients and add buttermilk mixture, stirring just until moistened. Fill muffin cups ¾ full.

Bake for 15–20 minutes. Cool for 5 minutes and remove from pan.

· CREAM CHEESE ·

This is our version of the delicious cream cheese muffins
we've all had at our favorite breakfast hangouts.

2 cups flour
¾ cup plus 3 tablespoons
   sugar, divided
1 ½ teaspoons baking powder
½ teaspoon baking soda
6 tablespoons butter, diced
1 cup buttermilk
3 tablespoons orange juice
1 tablespoon orange zest
1 egg
4 ounces cream cheese,
   cut into 12 cubes

Streusel topping
⅓ cup flour
3 tablespoons sugar
1 tablespoon orange juice
2 tablespoons butter, softened

Preheat oven to 400 degrees F. Spray muffin cups with nonstick cooking spray.

In medium bowl, combine flour, ¾ cup sugar, baking powder, and baking soda. With pastry blender or fork, cut in butter until mixture is crumbly.

In small bowl, whisk buttermilk, orange juice, orange zest, and egg together. Stir buttermilk mixture into dry ingredients just until moistened.

Fill muffin cups ¾ full. Dip each cube of cream cheese into remaining 3 tablespoons sugar and press into batter.

To make streusel, mix flour, sugar, orange juice, and butter together until crumbly. Spoon evenly over batter in muffin cups. Bake for 15–20 minutes. Cool for 5 minutes and remove from pan.

Note Store in refrigerator.

· SPICY CHOCOLATE ·

MAKES 12 MUFFINS

Blending chili, cinnamon, and chocolate together
gives this muffin an unusual flair.

2 cups flour
½ cup sugar
½ cup firmly packed brown sugar
¼ cup cocoa powder
2 teaspoons baking powder
1 teaspoon instant coffee
1 teaspoon chili powder
¾ teaspoon cinnamon
2 eggs
1 cup milk
1 tablespoon vinegar
⅓ cup butter, melted
1 teaspoon vanilla

Topping
3 tablespoons sugar
1 ½ teaspoons chili powder

Preheat oven to 400 degrees F. Spray muffin cups with nonstick cooking spray.

In large bowl, combine flour, sugars, cocoa, baking powder, instant coffee, chili powder, and cinnamon.

In medium bowl, whisk eggs, milk, vinegar, butter, and vanilla until blended. Stir into dry ingredients just until moistened. Fill muffin cups ¾ full.

For topping, combine sugar and chili powder in small bowl. Sprinkle topping mixture on batter in muffin cups.

Bake for 15–20 minutes. Cool for 5 minutes and remove from pan.

· CHEESE & CARAWAY ·

MAKES 12 MUFFINS

These cheesy muffins have a light rye taste
that complements heavier soups.

1³⁄₄ cups flour
¼ cup sugar
2½ teaspoons baking powder
¾ teaspoon salt
2 teaspoons caraway seeds
1 egg, well beaten
⅓ cup canola oil
1 cup milk
½ cup grated sharp processed
   American cheese
½ cup grated Swiss cheese

Preheat oven to 350 degrees F. Spray muffin cups with nonstick cooking spray.

Combine flour, sugar, baking powder, salt, and caraway seeds in large bowl.

In small bowl, combine egg, oil, and milk. Mix into dry ingredients just until moistened. Fold in cheeses.

Fill muffin cups ⅔ full. Bake for 15–20 minutes. Cool for 5 minutes and remove from pan.

INDEX

METRIC CONVERSION CHART

Volume Measurements		Weight Measurements		Temperature Conversion	
U.S.	Metric	U.S.	Metric	Fahrenheit	Celsius
1 teaspoon	5 ml	1/2 ounce	15 g	250	120
1 tablespoon	15 ml	1 ounce	30 g	300	150
1/4 cup	60 ml	3 ounces	90 g	325	160
1/3 cup	75 ml	4 ounces	115 g	350	180
1/2 cup	125 ml	8 ounces	225 g	375	190
2/3 cup	150 ml	12 ounces	350 g	400	200
3/4 cup	175 ml	1 pound	450 g	425	220
1 cup	250 ml	2 1/4 pounds	1 kg	450	230